Sally Schauman, with my best wishes,

Jay

The Cottingham Collection

The Cottingham Collection

Jay Appleton

The Wildhern Press 2008

Rear cover
Cottingham Church, drawn and supplied by Jill Carter

Front Cover
Jay and Iris Appleton beside Saltas del Rio Petrohue, Chile 1987.
From a photgraph by Mark Appleton.

Jay Appleton is an Emeritus Professor of Geography at the
University of Hull. His publictions include The Poetry of
Habitat, The Experience of Landscape and a collection of poems,
Grains Among the Chaff illustrated by Geoffry Shovelton.

Published by

The Wildhern press

131 High St.
Teddington
Middlesex TW11 8HH

1ˢᵗ Edition 2001
Copyright Jay Appleton 2001/8

ISBN 978-1-84830-075-0

THE COTTINGHAM COLLECTION

The medieval village of Cottingham lay at the eastern edge of the Yorkshire Wolds. Every winter the floodwaters of the River Hull washed against it on the eastern side, while the arable open fields lay on the rising ground to the west. All that has changed. The open fields have long been enclosed and the encroaching tide threatening it from the east is no longer that of the river but of the expanding urban sprawl of the City of Hull. Although its claim to be the largest village in England is no longer meaningful, (if it ever was), one is not supposed to say that in Cottingham, which has managed to retain something of a village atmosphere and is still a pleasant place to live in.

With the exception of the first poem, this little collection is not about Cottingham, though some neighbouring places, like Hull and Beverley, do appear. 'Centenary Sonnet', for example, was written for a celebration held in the Guildhall, Hull, (or, to give it its full name, Kingston-upon-Hull), on 13th May, 1999, to mark the seven hundredth anniversary of the granting of its Charter by Edward I. The link with Cottingham is the fact that all the poems were written within the parish, which has been the home of the writer for half a century. More famous poets have been here before, and Philip Larkin is buried in its cemetery.

The style of the poems is old-fashioned in that they scan and mostly rhyme, and I make no apology for that. There is a certain freedom which poetry achieves when it breaks away from the discipline of rhyme and meter, but there is also a price to be paid, and if ever we were to lose rhyming metrical verse altogether, some of the music would go out of the art of poetry.

CONTENTS

PRIVATE LINE TO COTTINGHAM

I have, no matter where I am,
A private line to Cottingham.
It isn't like a telephone,
This secret channel of my own;
It isn't like a wireless set;
It isn't like the Internet;
More like a feeling in the air
That Cottingham is always there.
It hasn't always been like this.
Norfolk was my idea of bliss,
A little village tucked away
Deep in the mists of yesterday.
The things which then attracted me
Still linger in the memory,
The village green, the local pub,
And Norwich City Football Club.
Though it had never crossed my mind
I'd leave those loyalties behind,
The old allegiance disappears,
Slowly receding down the years,
And though their treasured memory
Has never quite deserted me,
That private link with where I am
Has been transferred to Cottingham.
I've seen the streets of Samarkand,
I've trudged the shores of Zululand,
I've watched the Kiwi geysers blow,
I've breathed the air of Mexico,
Admired the slopes of Ararat
And the sharp teeth of Monserrat.
I've heard the roar of Iguassu,
I've sweltered in the desert too;

I've spanned the Globe, and everywhere
The feel of Cottingham is there.
Catullus, centuries ago,
Forged such a link with Sirmio,
Which, when he left the place behind,
Stayed in the forefront of his mind.
And though, in San Francisco Bay,
I feel a million miles away,
I flick the switch, and there I am,
Back home in dear old Cottingham.
Two special places in my heart
May lie ten thousand miles apart,
Or even more, but if instead
You were to look inside my head,
You'd find them, like a groom and bride,
Snuggling together, side by side.

THE IVY ON THE GARDEN WALL

The ivy on the garden wall
Reminds me of a waterfall.
Just as the white translucent veil
Throws patterns on the weathered shale,
So does the shiny green cascade
Mottle the brick with dappled shade.
Deep in the ivy's dark embrace
The blackbird finds a nesting-place,
A cosy refuge for her chicks
Between the foliage and the bricks.
The supple ivy branch entwines
In fluent *art nouveau* designs,
Whereas the mural markings are
Severely rectilinear.
Ivy is smooth and brick is rough;
They're made of very different stuff.
Green is the complement of red;
Ivy's alive and brick is dead.
The wall alone is cold and bare
Without the ivy clinging there,
Which never would be there at all
If unsupported by the wall.
Although they are so opposite
They seem to make the perfect fit,
Destined by circumstance to be
In symbiotic harmony.
Each partner can deliver what
The other partner hasn't got.
And so, whenever I recall
The ivy and the garden wall,
I marvel how they seem to be
A metaphor for you and me.

IF REASON RULED

If Reason ruled the universe alone,
Rational thought would govern our affairs;
But, as it is, she has to share her throne;
The wheat is thus polluted by the tares.
For in the world of stark reality
Her twin, Emotion, challenges her role,
Divesting her of her authority,
And robbing her of ultimate control.
We, the spectators of this sorry sight,
Commit ourselves with ostentatious pride
To Reason's cause, but in the ensuing fight
Are soon deserting to the other side.
When Reason thinks she has the final say,
Emotion summons *us* to bar her way.

SEEING STARS

The stars that stud the western sky
Are falling, falling, through the night;
Down, down they go, and by and by
Cross the horizon, out of sight.

The eastern constellations, though,
Are climbing unremittingly,
And rising, rising, up they go,
Propelled by senseless destiny.

Give me those friendly western stars
Which offer me no cause to fear.
Even the warlike planet, Mars,
Is soon condemned to disappear.

But when those stars and planets peep
Over the eastern parapet,
Into my private space they creep
Creating an unwelcome threat.

It little matters that I know,
With human rationality,
They have no will to come or go
And threaten my security.

And yet I readily conceive
The notion that they're watching me.
The magic power of make-believe
Is stronger than reality.

KNOCKING-ON-EIGHTY

Knocking-on-eighty! When I was a youth
Octogenarians, to tell the truth,
Were mostly bald, rheumaticky and bent
And, more than probably, incontinent.
Now suddenly I find it's time for me
To don the mantle of antiquity,
To creep around, arthritic, deaf and lame,
A ghost supported on a zimmer-frame.
My knees won't bend; backache has come to stay;
The ground looks nearly half a mile away.
'Knocking-on eighty' surely has to be
A certain formula for misery!

But when I stop and calmly think it through,
Eighty has many compensations too.
Of course I'll have to modify my style,
(And getting used to that may take a while),
Give up the things I'm not addicted to
And concentrate on what I want to do.
The things I used to live on as a boy,
Plain English cooking, I can still enjoy;
Hear symphonies I'd never heard before
And stack them safely in my treasure-store;
Rise with the dawn, inhale it clear and cold,
And watch the sky progress from green to gold.
After the passage of my fourscore years
A second childhood suddenly appears.
Grandchildren come and lead me by the hand
Into their own exclusive fairyland,
Where fiction and reality are one
And cynicism hasn't yet begun.

Through television I can still explore
The universe, just as I did before.
Thanks to the magic of photography
My eyes can reach the bottom of the sea,
Flit through the treetops, burrow in the sand,
Finding fresh challenges to understand.
After eight decades of experience
At last I find creation making sense.
Knocking-on-eighty, so it seems to me,
Is pretty well the perfect age to be!

HONI SOIT QUI MAL Y PENSE

Streaked with stale tears, but now, at last, asleep,
They came and laid you on my waiting breast;
Laid on me, too, a covenant to keep
Between us, understood if unexpressed.
I would provide a place for you to rest;
You would turn on the Sleeping Beauty's charms,
Spreading your little limbs to fill the nest
Made by an old man's woolly-sweatered arms.
It could not last. The gossip soon began.
No formal accusation: just a look.
'She is a girl', they said, 'and he's a man'.
They said no more; but that was all it took.
What have we done, that we have so defiled
A grandad's right to mend a broken child?

FULMODESTONE SEVERALS *

My bathroom window gave a sweeping view
Across the fields where wheat and barley grew,
And over on the far horizon stood
A dark, romantic, mesmerising wood,
Its rippled surface covered with a sheen
Of sunlit silver and of glossy green.
Above this undulating canopy
Rose here and there a more conspicuous tree
Standing majestic in the clear blue sky
To catch the wind and my observant eye.
Over the years these individual trees
Acquired distinctive personalities,
But all of them possessed one common trait,
An arrogant desire to dominate,
As every one asserted haughtily
Its self-proclaimed superiority.
The price they paid for standing so aloof
Was strict exclusion by the forest roof.
While you and I might stealthily invade
The silent woodland and its cooling shade,
From them the canopy contrived to hide
Whatever mysteries went on inside.
When Norman barons seized this Saxon land,
They showed the way to keep the upper hand,
And, in their pompous Norman-French, decreed
Their serfs to be a base, inferior breed.
Like Norman knights these domineering trees
Were upstart immigrants from overseas.
The Wellingtonia and the Douglas Fir
Were never meant to be transplanted here;
They'd have grown even taller staying on
In California or in Oregon.

What chance have any of our English trees
Against such fierce competitors as these?
The natives form an inconspicuous mass,
A large, amorphous, subjugated class.
Striving no less to penetrate the sky,
They reach a stature hardly half as high.
So does this sylvan aristocracy
Throw light upon our own society?
Are we, I wonder, governed by a breed
Genetically programmed to succeed?
And must we, like the oak, the ash, the beech,
Submit to tyrants way beyond our reach?

* The name of a wood in North Norfolk.

THE PRICE OF MOONLIGHT

We rightly praise the Sun-god in the sky,
Source of our light, our heat, our energy;
But do we ever pause to question why
The moon is so revered in poetry?
The truth is, when the dazzling day is done,
The thrifty moon retrieves a little bit
Of daylight from the abdicating sun,
Gilds it, dilutes it and re-cycles it.
Both play their own inimitable roles,
The savage *sol*, the gentler *clair-de-lune*;
But poets, lovers, all romantic souls
Stay loyal to that inefficient moon.
Light is like any scarce commodity,
More highly valued when in short supply.

ON THE EFFIGY OF A SAINT

Sling out this bland and sanctimonious thing
Which bears the name a better creature bore!
His eyes could watch the chisel chip away
Unwanted corners and his tongue could shape
An oath to match the hammer-blows. His heart
In obstinacy could outstare the stone.
In this mute monument his image stands,
Full face and profile, calipered to scale.
But where's the man who saw, who felt, who knew?
How, and by what strange path, has he escaped?
There is no sin, no Adam in a lump
Of oolitic limestone, no remorse,
No fears, no whims, no frailty and no fun.
A stern and retrospective sanctity
Has blanched the cheek that blushed with honest shame.
Let this cold carbonate of calcium
Stand justified before the Awful Throne
All burnished in obnoxious piety,
That, while the eyes of Heaven are turned on this,
The lovely lad that walked those windy hills
May leap the ladder, two-by-two, and squeeze
Under the curtain-flaps of Paradise.

PROSODECTOMY

You laugh at me because I waste my time
Writing my thoughts in meter and in rhyme.
You tell me that's what poets used to do
In days gone by, as if I didn't know.
'The formal rules of prosody', you say,
'Were made to suit the taste of yesterday;
'Popular writers of today, you'll find,
'Have left this verbal tyranny behind.'
Bring me a scalpel with your poetry
And let's perform a prosodectomy.
To make a poem, so the story goes,
You write a passage in poetic prose;
This done, continue to the second stage
And set it out perversely on the page.
Be resolute. Pull it about a bit.
The ways of doing this are infinite.
Though rules in general are not applied,
The left-hand margin may be justified,
But frequent aberrations from the rule
Are needed if you want to make it cool.
After the formal structure has been shed
We need some visual stimulus instead.
Indent a line, or even leave it out,
Or turn it upside down if you're in doubt.
never employ the upper case to do
the sort of things that i'd expect it to.

```
      the
       zig-zag
          is

            a

               useful
                  thing
                 to

                try
               if
             you're
             intention
          is
       to
         catch
          the
             eye.
```

But first we have to ostracise the rhyme.
It serves no purpose at the present day.
That was a narrow shave! But never mind;
The meter has to follow it down the
Drain.
Put all these principles into effect
     simultaneously
      and
        you
      will
      probably
    win
     an
      A
      W
      A
      R
      D

But all this innovation, I confess,
Is causing me intolerable stress,
So bear with my exasperation while
I retrogress to my accustomed style.
And when I've lost the skill to find a rhyme
Or make the meter flow in rhythmic time,
That's when I'll have to join the ranks of those
Who make their poems out of doctored prose.

NIGHT-TIME IN THE FENLAND

The Fenland when she wakes
Is bright with beet and barleycorn
And red, reposing roofs,
A comfortable ambience,
Not beautiful but prosperous,
Far as the eye can see.
But when she sleeps
She labours, restless, in a tide of dreams.

Come to the dyke,
This stark incision, mud-veneered;
Give up the sight to stranger things
And watch with me, and wait.
You see this web of pencil-lines
That rule the frames of earth,
Uncompromising, sharp and practical?
The crude diversities of hills
Are rolled to finer form,
And height has lost its horror.

Now, when the pinkish vapour-flecks
Grow greyed and jaded,
When the rich-rotting nightwaters
Are stirred and thickened,
And slowly start to surge,
Then the dead levels quicken and revive,
As fresh black blood
Brings to their pin-stripe arteries
The full primeval broth.

When the black silk,
The lining of the firmament,
Is fully drawn across,
Only the wind comes white.
Welcome him, windmill,
Creaking and squeaking,
Wheeling and beckoning,
Call to the pool,
'Slide, sluggard, slide
'Through the slits and through the slots,
'Out of the runnels and into the channels
'Bear down and slink away'.

It is never the breeze that sighs,
But the grey fenman swishing through the sedge
With furtive fowling-piece.
Stand stock still,
And let the fenman pass!

It is never the owl that flutes,
But the reed-rustling outlaw, whistling low,
And hollow night sustains the note
Across the misty moonlit plain
And many hundred years.
Stand stock still,
And let the fugitive float blindly by!

It is never a yard-hound
That howls about the poultry house,
But the mad monk of Ely
Spewing his curdled plainsong
Into the foggy haunting-ground

Of soft, brain-fevered shapes
And disembodied fears.
Stand stock still,
Lest the mad monk of Ely smell your soul
And hurl a cloud of gurgling peat
Between it and the east,
Where a new dawn, emerging yellow-green,
Shall render back the comfortable scene.

REPLY TO DYLAN THOMAS

Do not go gentle into that good night.
Rage, rage against the dying of the light.

Dylan Thomas.

Now that the race of life is nearly run
And morbid images of death appear,
I scornfully dismiss them one by one
And with them every resonance of fear.
No time for shedding a despondent tear!
Rather apply the test of common sense;
The roles of birth and death will then be clear -
Two focal points in one experience.
Nature endowed us with the will to live,
But also with the intellect to know
That any lease she condescends to give
Can only last until it's time to go.
Rage never stopped the dying of the light.
Why not go gentle into that good night?

LA SAGRADA FAMILIA, BARCELONA

The story of the Holy Family
Is told again in pinnacles of stone.
Gaudí achieves a novel symmetry,
Using the concept of the tapered cone.
The inspiration lies in Monserrat,
One of the great monastic sites of Spain,
A thousand metres of conglomerate
Carved into conic columns by the rain.
So do we turn to Christianity
To find what drove this enigmatic man,
Or is it simply in geology
We see the source of his amazing plan?
Perhaps the paradox is not so odd;
The hand of Nature *is* the hand of God!

THIS PLACE

This place has been here for a thousand years,
Changing, as people change, with passing time,
But basically as it now appears,
Romantic, charismatic and sublime.
There has evolved a kind of empathy
Between us, which the years cannot efface;
I have invested far too much of me
To snap the chain that binds me to the place.
At each encounter fragments of the scene
Have been ingested by my hungry mind;
And so, conversely, every time I've been,
Some part of me was always left behind.
I think, whatever may become of me,
This place will be my immortality.

THE ICING ON THE CAKE

Two-year-old Paul works on his birthday job.
He separates the icing from the cake,
Stuffs it assiduously in his gob
And leaves the rest for someone else to take.
His older brother's reached the second stage.
For him the years of babyhood are past.
Mature discrimination comes with age;
He's learnt to save the icing to the last!
But cake and icing, in the sight of God,
Are equals in the gastronomic game,
So, in this third and final period,
Eat them together; treat them both the same.
Although maturity *should* come with age,
I've never quite outgrown the second stage!

LET US NOT PAUSE TO THINK

Let us not pause to think, but, passing on,
Peep through the portholes of the sacred cow
At the raw ribs inside. Let us not read
With the unclouded eye of scholarship
The monumental writing in the sky,
But in the curtained cellars down the street
We'll crack the kernel of enlightenment.
The proud pretenders to philosophy
Distil the essence of the universe
And sniff the pungent droplets. But for us
The morning-evening shuttlecock shall fly
Through the slick round of brittle cameos;
Blue-flashing stones that punctuate the smoke
Of sociability, and with a beam
Arrest and hold an eligible eye;
And here the silky-fibred mist of hair
That bobs and trails and overpowers the sense;
And there the fragrance of a summer flower,
Aped in cheap chemicals and atomised
Among the herd of gauche and groovy bucks!
Time liberally lends its measured hours
To feed these trivialities in which
Is crystallised our continuity.
Come, you philosophers, and sweat it out
At this your peeping-hole. Some other time
Lend us your instruments to mensurate
The bounds of truth and beauty, but tonight
For pity's sake, let us not pause to think!

TO IRIS, FROM WARD 16, HULL ROYAL INFIRMARY

When what one values most seems least remote
And long familiarity prevails,
Appreciation then, it's time to note,
Must find some new expression, or it fails.
Sometimes a word is all that this entails,
A kiss, a touch, or just a certain look;
Yet I was often wanting in the scales,
Not man enough to bring myself to book.
If, on the other hand, by circumstance,
We find ourselves reluctantly apart,
What seems a hardship may prove just the chance
To rediscover what inflames the heart.
A sonnet's just another way to show
We really understand the truth we know.

... AND MELLOW FRUITFULNESS

The fog that drowns the motorway
Emasculates the sense of sight,
Creates one blank, diurnal night
And kills the beauty of the day.

As it invades the winter air,
The constant, unremitting strain
Tortures the eye, torments the brain
And turns contentment to despair.

When it encroaches on the sea
It rubs the sharp horizon out,
Plunges the sense of space in doubt
And substitutes perplexity.

But gentle mist, that spreads a skein
Across the images of things,
Softens their harsher forms and brings
An air of magic back again.

When in the street the lamps are lit
Sporadic pools of yellowed light
Confront the tyranny of night
And comfortingly challenge it.

Meadows, emerging from the night,
Their dewy cobwebs, one by one,
Gathering gold dust from the sun,
Entrap the misty morning light.

Bullrushes rising from the pond
And pampas grasses from the lawn,
Stretching their arms to greet the dawn,
Gain stature from the mist beyond.

The dying bonfire's smoky trail
Not quite a grey, not quite a blue,
But something in between the two,
Hangs in the woodland like a veil.

So never mind that foggy day.
If I can have my friendly mist,
Which no Romantic could resist,
It's but a paltry price to pay!

GOD BLESS THE WELSH

The Welsh are quite the nicest folk
A man could wish to know.
They treat the English as a joke,
Which only goes to show
They understand diplomacy;
They use it every day,
And that is why, presumably,
They always get their way.

You'll find them hiding in the hills
Or lurking in the vales.
They live on leeks and daffodils,
The staple food of Wales.
A language none can understand
They cherish jealously,
A mixture of saliva and
Explosive energy.

Those witches' hats the ladies wear
Are clearly meant to be
Suggestive of the mystic air
Of Celtic sorcery;
And if the image of a witch
Seems alien to the age,
They welcome pictures that enrich
Their culture's heritage.

Welsh men and women, so they say,
Have music in their veins,
Mendelssohn on a sunny day
And Wagner when it rains.

On Cader Idris in the spring
They serenade their sheep;
In Pontrhydfendigaid they sing
Messiah in their sleep.

From Swansea Bay to Talybont
There's rugby in the air,
And that's the only time you want
To handle them with care,
'Cos, win or lose, they're militant
With patriotic zest,
Insufferably arrogant
Or Celticly depressed.

So watch the Rugby Calendar,
And if they're due to play,
I've warned you what the problems are.
It's best to keep away!
Indulge their passion if you can,
And in a week or so
They'll be the nicest folk a man
Could ever wish to know.

SENSES OF PLACE

I ate a Scottish oatcake yesterday,
And I was in the Valley of the Spey.
I felt the breezes brushing through my hair,
And I was in the Valley of the Aire.
I listened to the blackbird's pretty tune,
And I was in the Valley of the Lune.
I smelt the fragrance of the elder flower,
And I was in the Valley of the Stour.
I saw the twinkle in my lady's eye,
And I was in the Valley of the Wye.
All the five senses surf the net for me,
Cleverly logging-on to *memory*.

CORRIDOR OF DREAMS

There is a passage in the shell of night
That leads beyond the clocks, beyond the reach
Of formal definition, full of round
Resounding echoes of familiar day.
Straightness and crookedness together meet
And light has lost its lucid property,
So that it touches only certain things
And leaves the rest unmade. Down the long line
A spongy, soft, nocturnal carpet creeps
To stun the resonance of those who tread
Its grey, uncharted ways. This is a place
Having no known and certain measurement,
But winding on and on. It is to me
A shadow-home, a cornered catacomb
Where earth-exhausted travellers can rest
And brood on half-reflected images.
In this interminable corridor
Are spacious, ashen halls and narrow wynds,
Dusty and mean and lined with apertures
That lead to little porches of a kind
Not seen by light-infected eyes. And I,
(Or rather that reflection of myself
Which represents my person at this court),
I trespass on this insubstantial stage,
And give such understanding to the part
I dare not call it dreaming. Through the dust
Float the quaint counterparts of living men.
Protean friends of sober, waking hours,
They swagger, self-assured and confident.
Other recesses, secret and apart,
Are unfrequented by night's populace.
In creaking cupboards, dark and undisturbed,

Feathery garments hang on polished pegs,
And common objects lie around the floor,
Abstracted from the roll of yesterday.
Infantile fears in cobweb corners skip
Like fascinating fawns, and in the dark,
Grey, embryonic figments of the mind,
Assuming partial form, retreat and lose
Even the semblance of their entity.
The record of ten thousand wasted days
Furnishes fragments to erect a scene
Of parody and imitative art.
And if one night proves longer than the rest,
And the strong stroke of retrogression fails,
Shall not the germ of feeling pulse its way
Down stranger, unsuspected galleries
And find delight in snatching certainty
From hitherto uncomprehended shapes?
But meanwhile in this stealthy peeping-show
By nightly visitation let the soul
Sample the flavour of eternity.

TO AN OLD WARDROBE

Faithful companion in a long campaign
Against the trials of advancing age,
We've stood together time and time again,
Knowing we have a common war to wage.
When I was young I'd calm my infant fears
Within your dark, enveloping recess.
Now, after fourscore memorable years,
We've each experienced a kind of stress.
And since I can no longer creep inside,
I know I've aged more rapidly than you
And realise I must be satisfied
With recollecting what I used to do.
It comforts me to think you'll carry on,
Old but defiant, after I have gone!

PHASELUS ILLE

Phaselus ille, quem videtis, hospites,
Ait fuisse navium celerrimus...

- Catullus IV.

That ship, my friends, which you are looking at,
Claims to have been the fastest thing afloat,
Whether with oar or sail insisting that
She triumphed over every other boat.
With this assertion every place agrees,
The wild, tempestuous Adriatic tide,
The scattered islands of the Cyclades,
Rhodes and Propontis on the Thracian side.
The forests of the Pontic Gulf concur,
For it was there on high Cytorus' brow
She dwelt, before they re-constructed her,
Designed and shaped her as you see her now.
Among the foliage rustling in the breeze,
Still unaware of what she was to be,
She shared her conversation with the trees,
Not yet equipped to venture on the sea.
Pontic Amastris knows it to be true,
Cytorus, clothed in box, can testify
That it was on those hills my vessel grew,
Her shapely timbers soaring to the sky.
In those deep waters first she dipped the blade;
From there she bore her master overseas,
Whether from left or right the Zephyrs played
Or Jove directed full astern the breeze.
And neither any promises nor vows
Were made to a terrestrial deity
When at the end she turned her ageing bows
To these still waters from the open sea.

But as her navigating days are past
And as her life of leisure now begins,
In sweet retirement she resides at last
And dedicates it to the Heavenly Twins.

GUINEA-PIG NIBBLING

Guinea-pig nibbling, nibbling hay,
What do you know of life?
Frittering fruitless hours away,
You and your nibbling wife?
Didn't you watch us snuggle her down
Under the mulberry tree?
Then why do you ask us where she's gone?
You know as much as we!

CENTENARY SONNET

KINGSTON-UPON-HULL:1299-1999

Providence dealt an inauspicious hand:
Waterlogged gravel, sand and silt and peat,
Two tides a day to inundate the land
Fringing the spot where Hull and Humber meet.
Far-sighted merchants on this lonely site
Laid the foundations of a thriving port;
Pile-drivers came to carry on the fight,
Feeling for solid rock to give support.
Faint-hearted folk would choose an easier place,
Looking for promise of a quick success;
It takes a sterner, more determined race
To civilise a marshy wilderness.
Through their inspiring perseverance we
Now celebrate this anniversary.

ULURU *

So there it is! A lifeless stranded whale?
An upturned hull drifting along the sand?
A slug, conceived on a gigantic scale?
A riddle, too obscure to understand?
The changing colours of the setting sun
Lend credence to an old ancestral myth;
Orange and red and purple, one by one,
Furnish a fantasy to conjure with.
For some this animistic legacy
From ancient times is palpably untrue;
'An arenaceous sedimentary'
Sums up for them the rock of Uluru.
But Science, thankfully, can never kill
The spirit of this charismatic hill!

* 'Ayers Rock' to the politically incorrect

CATECHISM

The morals of the adolescent me
Were guided through the swamps of puberty
By precepts formulated in a lore
Like regulations on a carriage door:
'Thou shalt not smoke nor spit nor pull the chain
'Nor stick thy head out of the bloody train'.
On this design my tutors based their brief
And wrapped my sins in Moses' handkerchief.
And while my infant feet were taught to tread
The straight and narrow path, my infant head
Was similarly channelled down a route
That by-passed forests of forbidden fruit,
Its tramlike course avoiding like the pox
Whatever failed to rank as orthodox.
And so I reached my twenties, green as grass,
A dull, respectable, conformist ass.
My children, in their more enlightened days,
Were shepherded in less restricted ways.
Seeking whatever goals appeared to please,
They gorged themselves on licensed heresies.
When in their turn they claimed the silver key,
I can't help wondering what they thought of me:
A wise, enlightened parent, or a sod
Who didn't seem to hear the voice of God.

WINDFARMING

The Windfarm! What's your policy
For generating energy?
I had an open mind until
They started one on Porter's Hill.
The Local Council, to a man,
Was solidly against the plan,
Declaring it would never do
To desecrate the lovely view,
But ultimately came the day
When innovation got its way.
I went to see what they had done
And found they'd just erected one,
A single column rising high
Into the clear September sky.
Three blades as bright as stainless steel
Mimicked the motion of a wheel,
Emitting as they whirled around
An intermittent swishing sound.
The sight of this machinery
Had a profound effect on me.
I thought 'Utility apart,
'It's quite a stunning work of art,
'And all this prejudicial fuss
'Is patently ridiculous!'
When next I went to Porter's Hill
I found the turbine working still,
But by its side another one
Had now appeared to join the fun,
And by and by, upon my word,
They'd started putting up a third.
Over the months they added more,
In toto twenty-bleeding-four!
Now Porter's Hill's a dreadful sight!
A paragon of visual blight!

Everyone knows Trafalgar Square.
Last night I dreamt that I was there.
A thousand tourists also went
To see the Nelson Monument.
But presently I chanced to spy
Out of the corner of my eye
A replica in Whitehall and
Another half-way down the Strand.
Suddenly all along The Mall
Were statues of the Admiral
And half a dozen more again
Strung out along Saint Martin's Lane.
The whole West End had now become
A sort of 'Nelsonarium'.
The ghost of Nelson thundered down:
'Look what they've done to London Town!
'As long as I was here alone
'Up on my pigeon-plastered throne,
'The British public treated me
'With deferential courtesy,
'But now I'm just a laughing-stock,
'And all they do is come to mock!
'In short, a unitary thing
'Which people find enrapturing
'Can generate antipathy
'When seen in multiplicity.
'Apply the lesson, if you will,
'To what they've done on Porter's Hill;
'Remind them of this simple fact,
'It's best to think before you act!'

NICHOLAS PAUL

(To a new grandson)

This little pulse of life that lies
Encradled in his cosy cot,
Content to close his sleepful eyes,
Prompts me to contemplate his lot.

I know your mum, I know your dad,
Your sister and your brother too;
You couldn't be a luckier lad,
Having them all to cherish you.

But what you'll do, and what you'll be,
And who you'll meet, and where you'll go:
These things, which mean so much to me,
I don't suppose I'll ever know.

So now, for just an hour or two,
I'll sit and watch you, little man.
I'll let the Lord look after you
And just enjoy you, while I can.

EMILY KATE

(To a new granddaughter)

Life offers no experience
Quite like the miracle of birth,
That moment when we each commence
Our pilgrimage through Planet Earth.

Right from that first perplexing day
When you appeared in Naremburn,
Starting on Life's demanding way,
It was your destiny to *learn*.

When as a child I learnt to look,
To wonder and to understand,
I opened nature's story-book
In England's green and pleasant land.

As you begin to learn the art
You'll have a different book to use.
Your *Nature Notes* are sure to start
With gums, galahs and kangaroos.

A different world will open out
Before your keen, enquiring eye,
As you begin to ask about
The 'what?', the 'wherefore?' and the 'why?'.

I used to watch the Northern Star;
It held me captive in its spell;
But I imagine, where you are,
The Southern Cross will serve as well.

I waited forty years or so
To smell the legendary gums -
A fragrance you will surely know
Before your second birthday comes.

Although you live so far away
On that remote Australian shore,
Thinking about you every day
Just makes us love you all the more.

PROSPECT AND REFUGE

When walking on the mountain track,
A silhouette against the sky,
I need no trees to shield my back
And screen me from some prying eye.

If those anxieties begin
Which travellers are subject to,
I look for re-assurance in
The panoramic field of view.

No hazard can endanger me,
No hurt can take me by surprise,
As long as I can clearly see
The places where they might arise.

But if I'm in the valley's shade,
Sauntering by the riverside,
I need the comfort of the glade
To offer me a place to hide.

The creatures living in the wood,
The deer, the rabbit and the fox,
Master the friendly neighbourhood,
Its trees, its bushes and its rocks.

For them the woodland can provide
In infinite variety
Places to see, places to hide,
So, if for them, why not for me?

We blind each other with the thought
That we are we and they are they,
Though, as the sciences have taught,
We share a common ancestry.

Whether we walk the windy hill
Or wander through the friendly trees,
We find ourselves employing still
The old survival strategies.

THE RAIN IN SPAIN

'*The rain in Spain stays mainly on the plain.*'
What an outrageous piece of sophistry!
Meteorologists protest in vain
At such a manifest absurdity.
So fiction gets away with it again!
The pen is mightier than geography!

LOOS IN THE NIGHT

A man's godda do what a man's godda do.
It's twenty to three and I'm off the loo.
The last time I went it was twenty to two,
But a man's godda do what a man's godda do!

IMAGINATION

The far horizon forms a boundary-line
Encompassing the landscape I can see,
Which makes it feel conspicuously mine,
A sort of visual private property.
But I've another special kind of eye,
Located somewhere deep within the brain.
It sees what lies beneath that distant sky,
Which only speculation can attain.
Science is like our ordinary eye;
It reads the world with crystal clarity,
But ultimately it's restricted by
The limits of its own capacity.
Religion and the arts are free to stray
Beyond that fence where science has to stay.

EVENING AT SAINT PANCRAS STATION

(Health warning: to be read by railwaymaniacs only)

A line of locos, groomed to venture forth,
A vault above, a haze of steam below,
The mouth of London, gaping to the north -
This was Saint Pancras sixty years ago.
A feeble sunbeam from the setting sun
Invades the pall of dirty yellow light,
Alighting on commuters, one by one,
Who go to face the suburbs and the night.
Each train, a locomotive at its head,
Will soon ascend the bank to Kentish Town,
While southbound trains in gleaming 'midland red'
Negotiate the gradient coming down.
Plato depicted two realities,
A kind of essence, spirit or ideal,
And then the solid counterpart of these,
Material images which make them real.
And so it seems to be with railway lines.
They too express a true identity,
A strange, elusive 'something' which defines
A kind of 'Midland' personality.
For us, who are obsessed with railway lore,
The line's a story waiting to be told,
Like music on the pages of a score
Ready for some conductor to unfold.
So every time we watch a train arrive
Here in the twilight of the dying day
Saint Pancras suddenly becomes alive
With places it encountered on the way.
The various stations it was passing through
Have yielded up their personalities.

Sheffield is here, Trent Junction, Leicester too,
Familiar friends and old acquaintances.
Euston, with all its classic elegance,
Was vandalised by brash modernity.
King's Cross has never really had the chance
To match its gothic neighbour's dignity.
How different is the mood of Paddington!
It draws on quite another treasure-chest
By sampling what the great Brunel had done.
Its poetry comes wholly from the West.
Saint Pancras Station, then, is simply what,
As individuals, we choose to see.
Some call this masterpiece of Gilbert Scott
A Mid-Victorian monstrosity!
So when I'm in a 'Midland' frame of mind,
Watching these snaking carriages awhile,
The ghost of Derby will be sure to find
A mouthpiece in this Neo-gothic pile.
The notion that a building can ingest
The moods of places is ridiculous.
We know! But leave us to our harmless jest
In this, my favourite London Terminus!

WHO DARES?

Who dares to wake
To the wide-acred prison of a world
Made white with wind and sunshine and equipped
With all the tangibility of things?
To watch the substance grow from shade to shape,
To bump and bounce among the pins, and tread
The creaking cobweb of mortality?
Whetting his wisdom on a bruising-stone
Is rich reward for him who dares to wake.

Who dares to sleep,
Pledging his spirit to oblivion
In the great hall of night, and, when the sun
Wakes up, redeem from pawn another self?
Perhaps some shooting-star has sparkled off
The tinder of a vision and revived
With brilliant show the blind, bat-shadowed hours.
The coffers of the moonbeam-gods are filled
With moonbeam-gold for him who dares to sleep.

Who dares to die?
To walk the windy cloister of beyond?
Better to brave the sanctity of sleep
Than whine and whimper like a tired child
An hour beyond his little dreaming-time!
The dreams of life are viable with hope
For him who dares to plant them in the grave;
And if they shoot and grow beyond the fence,
Let him enjoy the fruit who dares to die!

CUPRESSUS LEYLANDII

The Leyland Cypress is a tree
Everyone loves to hate.
To kindle animosity
Appears to be its fate.

Its all-obliterating shade,
Its freely wandering roots -
These attributes are tailor-made
For boundary disputes.

Shedding its dessicated leaves
And spreading them around,
It surreptitiously achieves
The poisoning of the ground.

The cypress, then, in many ways
Is justly vilified,
But every coin, the proverb says,
Must have another side.

If trees are planted in a row
Then quite predictably
A hedge will ultimately grow
And reach maturity.

Of course the neighbours will complain
Of lost amenities;
They'll say it's driving them insane
And blame it on the trees.

When dogs behave indecently
The owners get the blame,
So why should not this guiltless tree
Be treated just the same?

A Leyland Cypress on its own
Is quite a different thing.
A site on which it stands alone
Is much more flattering.

In April when they shoot anew
And trees are vivid green,
They owe their fine proportions to
The spaces in between.

So personally I deplore
This urge to denigrate.
I have a strong affection for
The tree they love to hate.

The pundits, then, may scheme away
To have this tree disgraced,
But who, I ask myself, are they
To criticise my taste?

I love the cypress soaring high
To catch the morning sun;
So bully for *Leylandii!*
Let's plant another one!

NARROWBOAT

The River Aire at Knottingley
Was where we went to cruise.
It flows to Chapel Haddlesey
And on to join the Ouse.
With one hand on the tiller and
The other on the Morse,
I took the narrowboat in hand
And steered a crooked course.

The River Aire at Knottingley
Is wildly serpentine.
Look at the map and you will see
It's just a wiggly line.
'Take yer bends wide!', the lady said,
'And steady as yer go!'
So down the river, full ahead,
I swung her to and fro.

The lurid clouds looked threatening,
The wind was rising high.
A sheet of rain came plummeting
Out of the angry sky.
I buttoned up my anorak,
Put on my hat again;
Gritted my teeth and settled back
To face the driving rain.

The cabin looked inviting, but
The door was open wide;
So, just before I pushed it shut,
I took a peep inside.

My friends were talking down below
And keeping warm and dry,
While, shivering from head to toe,
And getting drenched, was I.

As round those sinuosities
We swept from side to side,
I kept recalling memories
Of what I'd seen inside;
A sense of peace and harmony
Pervaded everywhere -
A capsule of serenity
Careering down the Aire!

My aim is not in any sense
To grumble or complain.
It's part of the experience
To feel the wind and rain;
But pictures of tranquility
Kept going through my head,
And, symbol of pure luxury,
The pillow on my bed.

So then, in my appointed place
Up on the afterdeck,
With raindrops coursing down my face
And trickling down my neck,
Negotiating every bend
This thought occurred to me:
'We need both parties to contend,
'Storm and tranquility!'

The bottom bunk is slotted in
A dark and deep recess,
And, dreaming of it, I begin
To sense its cosiness;
And when we're safely through the lock
At Chapel Haddlesey,
Securely moored by nine o'clock,
That bed will be for me!

PER ARDUA AD ASTRA

If Wilbur Wright or Orville were alive,
If Louis Blériot were still around,
If Brown and Alcock somehow could contrive
To visit their historic stamping-ground,
Imagine their amazement when they found
Four hundred passengers with all their gear
Cruising at just below the speed of sound
And practically in the stratosphere.
They'd marvel at the miracle of flight,
They'd rave at how ambitious we had got,
Serving at that intimidating height
A three- or four-course dinner piping hot.
Yet here's an even more astounding thing -
People complain about the catering!

FISHY BUSINESS

I see you hiding under there,
You funny little trout.
You seem to have forgotten where
Your tail is sticking out!

Under the lily-pad you spend
The sultry summer day,
Oblivious of your other end
Which gives the game away.

I wouldn't want to injure you,
But, yes, I understand
Your coyness is responding to
A natural command.

It may appear we're playing at
A rather different game,
But how we view our habitat
Is pretty much the same.

I'd make a jolly useful fish
If fate should so decree,
Because, like you, I wouldn't wish
To lose my privacy.

If I were in your scaly skin
Slithering through the reeds,
I'd find a pool to settle in
Among the waterweeds.

I think it likely you'd agree,
If only you could speak,
That life is just, for you and me,
A game of hide and seek.

If you allowed a stealthy pike
To sidle up too near,
I know exactly what it's like,
That nauseating fear.

We need to watch the world around,
While keeping out of sight;
Though different menaces abound,
We need to get it right.

With my imagination I
Can penetrate your lair.
I think I know the reason why
You seem contented there.

But one thing which a fish could not
Begin to understand
In twenty thousand years is what
It's like to live on land!

CREDO FOR FOUR VOICES

Primus:
Two thousand years the road is long
And no-one knows how wide;
The host proceeds, a myriad strong,
And I must turn aside.

For if there be a Paradise,
And if there be a God,
I'll seek them with unblinkered eyes
And I shall choose the road.

The faithful flock of Christendom
The thinking mind abhor;
Better be blinded and become
More faithful than before.

Locked in the steepled vessel's womb
They seek the insipid realm,
A prelate in the engine-room,
A bishop at the helm.

Proclaim your evidence in court,
Intone it every day,
Provided it be never thought
To point the other way.

Secundus:
A midnight necromancer stands
Before the altar-stone;
With spiny, sacrilegious hands
He beckons the unknown.

But see! This horrified divine
Defeats his purpose grim;
With counter-cabbalistic sign
He outmanoeuvres him.

Then to his thwarted, impious foe
The father turns, surprised,
'What fiend was that? For I would know
'Whom I have exorcised!'

Before the windows of the grave
Still hangs the impervious blind.
Furious the jealous elders rave
At those who peep behind.

The prophets of antiquity
Once chronicled the true;
No infidel cartography
Shall map the ground anew.

Tertius:
Take heed, Columbus, ere your boat
You launch upon the main,
Where bloody-minded monsters float
Beyond the Pope's domain.

Here at the margins let us pause
Before we pass the gate;
Beware the crisp, serrated jaws
That flash and yawn and wait!

What tempts a man in heresy
To hazard what he hath?
The candles of conformity
Shall light the proper path.

For we are marked for Paradise,
So shall it be our lot
To hear the damned, despairing cries
Of those that roast and rot!

Quartus:
The poisoned shafts of argument
Fly random through the night;
Each on its puny purpose bent
Contaminates the light.

And in this timeless church I sit
And pray, I know not what,
For I have half remembered it
And I have half forgot.

But though the clarity of truth
My grasping hand elude,
The limping loyalties of youth
Temper the godless mood.

So let the sceptic shake his head,
And let the cynic sneer;
Until the flower of faith be dead
The heart shall worship here.

FELLWALKING

As I was walking once on Langdale Fell
They taunted me 'When you are old and grey
'The ravages of age will start to tell;
'You'll have to put your walking boots away.'
Well, here I am, and only yesterday
I climbed the grinding path by Rossett Ghyll,
On over Hanging Knotts I fought my way;
Beyond Esk Hause, higher and higher still;
Over Broad Crag and on to Scafell Pike,
Standing at last on England's highest place.
There, at the culmination of the hike,
I felt the breath of nature on my face,
Drank the west wind, imbibed the mountain air,
Snug by the fireside in an easy chair.

TRIO IN E FLAT MAJOR, (D929)

There is a haunting tune that Schubert wrote.
It conjures up a haunting scene for me,
Which seems to match the music, note for note;
Two images in perfect harmony.
A leafy foreground, dark and shadowy,
Leads forward to a more expansive space
Crowned by a dense arboreal canopy
Which lends a sense of safety to the place.
But strict confinement brings anxiety
And through the trees the eye can carve a way
In search of freedom, space and liberty,
Past purple mountains to the dying day.
Why Schubert has this strange effect on me
I'm quite content to call a mystery.

ELGAR'S WORCESTERSHIRE

The Worcester Beacon is the place to go
To see the English landscape at its best.
The Severn Valley spreads itself below,
Backed by the Cotswolds' all-embracing crest.
To the north-east white plumes of smoke betray,
Beyond the skyline, Blake's satanic mills.
To the north-west one catches, far away,
A glimpse of Housman's blue remembered hills.
Out to the west the Cambrian Mountains rise
Beyond the foothills of Montgomery,
While to the south the sigmoid Severn lies
And slowly widens to become the sea.
Worcester Cathedral rises from the trees.
Tewkesbury Abbey, Malvern Priory
And churches less conspicuous than these
Mark out the heart of each community.
When Elgar set about the happy task
Of giving us his songs, his symphonies,
Was this the raw material, I ask,
From which he built those 'English' melodies?
Were those the fields where Nimrod joined the chase,
That mighty hunter, fast and furious?
Could that half-timbered farmhouse be the place
Which housed the death-bed of Gerontius?
Just as that landscape captivates the eye,
So Elgar's music captivates the ear.
On Worcester Beacon, halfway to the sky,
Worcestershire's what I see, but Elgar's what I hear.

MIDDLETON HALL *

The trellised pattern of converging streams
Carved up the woodland into secret cells,
Sparked off in Paxton's eye romantic dreams,
Who cast on Middleton arcadian spells.
A chain of lakes mirrored the summer sky;
Expansive prospects crowned each grassy plain;
A new-conceived creation by-and-by
Woke into life - and fell asleep again.
But, once the old design had been effaced,
Possessive nature seized the residue
Till more ambitious notions were embraced
And grander visions shaped the ground anew.
So Middleton becomes for botany
The Flagship of the Principality!

* Middleton Hall, in Carmarthenshire, is the site of the National
Botanic Garden of Wales, created to celebrate the Millenium.

THE ODIOUS MISTER WHITE

Beside our house there used to be
A little piece of Arcady,
A meadow where the rabbits played
Under a chestnut's friendly shade,
And I would sit and watch the sheep
While Edward had his Sunday sleep.
For years we lived contentedly
In this idyllic scenery
Until the odious Mister White
Acquired it as a building site.
As we envisaged rows and rows
Of ghastly little bungalows
Edward and I resolved to fight
The execrable Mister White,
And scotch the diabolic plan
Of that abominable man.
But ultimately, to our cost,
Somehow we tragically lost.
With incantations every night
We cursed the odious Mister White.
Theresa Troutbeck came to tea
Looking for mutual sympathy.
'My dear, what dreadful news!' she cried,
'We'll have to get him certified!
'You know he's building them *to let?*
'I can't imagine who we'll get!
'My dear, the riff-raff and the scum
'Will turn the place into a slum.
'That man has never understood
'The *ethos* of the neighbourhood!'

But this was seven years ago,
And bricks mature and gardens grow.
Beneath those newly planted trees
Are flower beds and shrubberies.
To lose the meadow was a curse,
Yet I'll admit it could be worse.
The architecture's not too bad;
Innocuous if a trifle 'trad',
And, with the gardens fresh and green,
It's better than it might have been.
As for the neighbours, truth to tell,
We seem to manage pretty well.
The little chap from Number One
Is just a cuddly ball of fun;
Although we think he's only three
He's quite hilarious company!
He tells my husband everything,
Which Edward finds quite flattering.
The folk who live at Number Two
Were angels when we had the 'flu;
Charles cut the grass and fetched the coal
And Brenda made a casserole.
A widow lives at Number Three;
Cats are her speciality,
And when we have to go away
She'll feed Jemima every day.
The man we call The Commodore
Has just moved in at Number Four.
He's not a proper naval man;
He just goes sailing when he can,
And though we hardly know him yet
I'm bound to say he looks a pet.

In short, the neighbours we have got
Have proved a most congenial lot.
We thought we'd like to celebrate
This unexpected turn of fate,
And Edward said 'The thing to do
Is organise a barbecue.'
We've fixed it for tomorrow night;
And - we've invited Mister White!

Jay Appleton

BIRDS

If ever I should chance to write
A book on ornithology,
I think I'd choose the mode of flight
To classify the species by.

First there are birds that thrash the air
With fierce, phrenetic energy.
Their tiny winglets disappear
From human visibility.

The little wrens, the humming-birds,
The tits, and even smaller things,
Creatures too miniscule for words
Appear to be devoid of wings.

The blackbird and the mistlethrush
In rhythmic regularity
Fly purposefully from the bush
With metronomic constancy.

But if we take the albatross,
Wing-flapping goes against the grain;
With pinions several yards across
It's nature's fixed-wing monoplane.

The buzzard, too, has rigid wings.
A thousand feet above the ground,
Searching for little furry things
It circles round, and round, and round.

Pigeons, performing a display,
Will flap their wings compulsively,

Then cut the engine, so to say,
And glide away contentedly.

The rook that fights the windy day
Climbs up the shoulder of the gale,
Spectacularly falls away
And sails, triumphant, down the vale.

Some birds just flop their way along.
The heron, nesting in the trees,
The plover, with its 'peewit' song,
Are representative of these.

The sea-birds, perching on the cliff,
In suicidal nesting-sites,
Go zooming out to sea, as if
They never knew the fear of heights.

The gannet is a special case;
He flies along deceptively,
Then, plunging at a gathering pace,
He spears the surface of the sea.

Canada geese, in echelon,
Display a different way to fly,
As, cruising home, they sail along,
Formation-dancing in the sky.

So did the pundits get it right
With all their slick taxonomy?
If they had watched the birds in flight
They might have done it differently!

O LITTLE TOWN OF FAKENHAM

O little town of Fakenham,
How still we see you lie!
Above your deep East Anglian sleep
The silent years go by.
Yet I can still imagine you
Just as you used to be
When you were in your middle age,
I in my infancy.

Those were for me the halcyon years
When you were at your best;
One railway station in the east,
Another in the west.
The Town and Country Planning Act
Was many years away,
And property developers
Had yet to have their day.

Though Fakenham was always an
Attractive little town,
It had two small deficiencies
Which sadly let it down;
I always had a craving for
The mountains and the trees,
And Fakenham, regrettably,
Was rather short of these.

One night I dreamt of Fakenham
Just as it used to be.
The layout of the town was quite
Familiar to me,

Except that, on the northern side,
Obscuring half the sky,
Arose a monumental hill
A thousand metres high.

I climbed this eminence to see
The panoramic view,
Astonished at the landscape which
I always thought I knew.
The legacy of Townshend and
The heritage of Coke
Had disappeared by sorcery
As in a story-book.

The ploughlands and the meadows of
The cultivated plain
Were covered with a canopy
Of forest once again.
Could the subconscious be at work
Attempting to provide
The hills and woods that Fakenham
Had always been denied?

The placid River Wensum still
Meanders much the same.
The gasworks in retirement has
Achieved immortal fame.
The medieval parish church
Still dominates the town
Which property developers
Are turning upside down.

So when I picture Fakenham
Seventy years ago,
I wonder if it really is
The place I used to know;
Or am I just imagining
The details I recall?
Perhaps the town of Fakenham
Was never there at all!

ON HEARING VERDI'S *REQUIEM* IN BEVERLEY MINSTER

When I reflect on how this church began,
This masterpiece of medieval man,
It seems bizarre such high technology
Should go with such a crude theology.
Was it a work of love, or was it built
To expiate the world's collective guilt,
To please a hard, vindictive god, intent
On retribution, fear and punishment?
Beyond those pillars with their massive girth
Stands Verdi's representative on earth;
Raising his baton on this hallowed ground
He conjures up a miracle of sound.
A falling triad in a minor key
First sets a mood of deep tranquility,
And rich, romantic harmonies suggest
Perpetual light and everlasting rest.
But soon the music rises to a swell,
Ushering in a prescience of hell.
A taut, gigantic drum comes into play
For thumping out the dread of Judgment Day.
The saved are herded to celestial light;
The damned consigned to everlasting night.
Though, for a building of this early date,
Plainsong would surely be appropriate,
It takes a music of a different kind
To penetrate the medieval mind,
And, for a moment, I begin to see
The beauty of its stark simplicity.
I know that, in the sober light of day,
The fire will die, the magic pass away,

And pictures of that drama in the sky
For me once more will fail to satisfy.
Biblical myths and images we find
Are too simplistic for the modern mind,
But still retain the power to impress,
If fitted out in operatic dress.
Music and architecture now combine
To turn prosaic water into wine.
Two strikingly contrasting kinds of art,
Stylistically centuries apart,
Can, for a time, re-generate for me
A halfway house to credibility.

CLOUDS IN THE SUNSET

Clouds in the sunset, like old men, go grey.
They cannot keep the glory that they had.
Losing the peacock colours of the day
They grow anaemic, negative and sad.
And we, who watch the golden sunset die
And deprecate the passing of the light,
Plead with the garish colours of the sky
Not to surrender to the impending night.
A greying cloud remains the shape it was,
As greying friends are still the folk we knew,
But has to let the sunset go, because
The evening has a kind of magic too.
Sporting the colours of the afternoon,
How could a cloud do justice to the moon?

Printed in the United Kingdom
by Lightning Source UK Ltd.
131803UK00001B/61-102/P